GOD'S HEALING MEDICINE

DAILY SCRIPTURES FOR FAITH AND MIRACLES

SECOND EDITION

BY:

REV. JOAN M. BROWN

Covenant Freelance Services
Green Valley, Arizona

God's Healing Medicine
Daily Scriptures For Faith And Miracles

Second Edition, Revised © February 2026
Copyright © 2004, 2026 Rev. Joan M. Brown, Covenant Freelance Services
All rights reserved worldwide

Unless otherwise indicated, all Hebrew and Greek word definitions in this volume are from:
Strong's Exhaustive Concordance, James Strong, 1890
Brown, Driver, Briggs Hebrew Lexicon
Thayer's Greek Lexicon

Library of Congress Control Number: 2026901158
ISBN-978-0-9706661-5-4

First edition 2004
Second edition 2026
Printed in the United States of America

Cover Image: Joan M. Brown/Canva.com

Publisher:
Covenant Freelance Services
472 N. Ramos Lane
Green Valley, AZ 85614
USA

DEDICATION

෨

This book is dedicated to my husband, Ed
my partner and friend
who has supported me in ministry
and sacrificed of my time throughout this project.

A special thanks to:

My parents
Martin and Katherine Arendt
Who have raised me in the fear of the Lord,
have been godly examples in my life,
who believe in me, and have supported
and encouraged me in every endeavor I have undertaken.

Rev. Rebecca Hamming
Step of Faith Ministries; Paw, Paw, Michigan
My sister-in-law, mentor, and friend,
Who has tutored me throughout my Christian walk.
Her faith in my ability and support of my ministry
has enabled me to pursue God's call on my life.

Sister Brenda Ervin
CEO of Barndoor Publishing; Grand Blanc, Michigan
A fellow author, Christian sister, and personal friend,
For her prayers, encouragement,
and advice throughout the writing process.

Rev. Jerry Pruett
Davison Full Gospel; Davison, Michigan
Who provided my spiritual covering as well as
mentoring and encouraging me in personal ministry.

Sister Lola Byrd
My mentor and confidant
Whose command of the Word of God
has motivated me to greater heights in the Lord.

Rev. Charles Fowler
Believer's Fellowship of Colorado; Colorado Springs, Colorado
For his kind assistance in critiquing my biblical Greek.

CONTENTS

••

FOREWORD

"Originally published in 2004, the truths in this book saved my life. In 2008, I was miraculously healed after a diagnosis of colon cancer."

Ed Brown
Delphi Electrical Engineer, Retired

"Joan's passion and calling as a bible teacher and writer is evident. Her insightful book and teaching is excellent and powerfully reflects God's hand on her life. "

Brenda Ervin
CEO, Barndoor Publishing

"God's people should be aggressive to follow His directions and take His medication, His Word! I pray you will allow your spirit man to meditate on the truth in these pages."

Rev. Rebecca Hamming
Step-Of-Faith Ministries

PREFACE

My Personal Faith Journey

I am still on the great journey of faith. I, too, am learning to walk it out, like father Abraham who the scripture says took steps of faith (Romans 4:12). I used to try to answer questions about why people who seemed to have faith, died anyway. That is a loaded question as there could be a multitude of reasons. Some people have faith only in their head and not their heart. Some started too late. The sickness or disease was so powerful that it became a race against time. They simply were not able to get enough Word into their heart fast enough. Others short circuit the process with their own mouth. Some things we will never understand this side of heaven. I don't contemplate other people's circumstances anymore. I was thinking about it one day and the Holy Spirit brought Hebrews 11:6 to my mind.

"Without faith it is impossible to please God."

I realized I had to ask myself one question. Why am I trying to walk by faith? Am I trying to walk by faith because the pastor says it's the thing to do, or because the great faith teachers say so? Is it because I want a new car, or a million dollars, or because I need healing? Or, is it because my heart's desire is to please God and He said I can't please Him otherwise? This walk of faith cannot be results oriented. It will produce results. But, my orientation must be my love for Jesus and my desire to please God.

I choose to walk by faith because the alternative, doubt and unbelief, displeases God. Not for any other reason. My decision is no longer 'results dependent.' It doesn't matter to me anymore who fails or who succeeds. It doesn't matter if I ever perfect it. It doesn't matter whether I see another result for the rest of my life. I will still pursue this walk of faith because it pleases God. I'll bet that's why Jesus did it. Jesus, the Word Himself, had to learn the Word the same way we do. He acted on every bit of truth He found and He only had the Old Testament. In the Old Testament the book of Habakkuk contrasts pride with faith. It says,

"Behold, his soul which is lifted up is not upright in him: but the just shall live by his faith."

I've made my decision. If God's Word says it, I believe it, and that settles it. I've made my decision. You must make yours.

INTRODUCTION

Knowledge + Faith = "X" (X being any factor of The Blessing)
Healing is one factor of The Blessing
Therefore: Knowledge + Faith = Healing

God, Himself, tells us in His Word that our problems are due to a lack of knowledge. You must know what God's Word says about healing in order to receive it. That knowledge combined with your faith in His Word will achieve the result you desire. In this case it is healing. In this earthly realm sickness is a fact. However, God's Word is Truth. Here's the good news. Truth can change any fact controlled by the curse.

I would not tell anyone they should not go to the doctor. Doctors are very committed to healing which is directly in line with God's will. Sometimes an accident or attack comes so suddenly you are not in a position to resist on your own. Thank God for the prayers of other saints and for doctors who can keep us alive until we can get to a place where we are strong enough to resist sickness and disease on our own.

I will tell you that our God has made provision for your healing. It comes through His Word combined with your Faith in that Word. Many people are in different stages of faith development. You should ALWAYS pray and consult God about what you are to do in any given situation; and let the Holy Spirit, your inward witness, guide you. The Holy Spirit knows your situation as well as how much Word is effectively working in you. Today you may have enough faith for healing with the doctor's help. Next year, you may not even need the doctor. It is God's desire for you to come to a place of faith where you can receive your healing directly by His Word. This book will help you in your faith journey.

Whatever you do, use all the faith you have when you do it. That is how faith is developed. Always believe and understand that God is the true healer no matter whose hands it comes through. Give Him the glory!

Note: This book is a revised edition of its first publication in 2004. It has a new subtitle, an added foreword, and minimally revised content.

THE WHOLE MAN

CHAPTER ONE

HUMAN DYNAMICS
(Spirit, Soul & Body)

Man is a unique creation. Regardless of what evolutionists would have you believe, man is a created being. Man is created in the image and likeness of God. That is what gives man his ability to create. No other creature has the abstract ability to create. God is the master creator and the man he formed, in his likeness, bears His ability to create, albeit on a much smaller scale.

Scripture tells us God is a tripartite being, meaning He is three persons in one. Well, God made man in His image and likeness. Man is also a tripartite being. Man is comprised of spirit, soul, and body. Your body is your physical self. Your soul is that part which makes you uniquely you. It is your mind (intellect), will, emotions and personality. Your spirit is the real you that will live for eternity. It is God's breath in you. Your spirit man was created in God's image. God is a spirit being. Your spirit gives you the ability to communicate and fellowship with God. It is the link between the created and the creator.

Think of it like this: you are a spirit, you have a soul, and you live in a body.

Before the fall, Adam could easily use his spirit to walk and talk with God in the Garden of Eden. After the fall the link between man's soul and spirit was broken. Not only did Adam's sin cause the process of physical death to begin, it caused immediate spiritual death. Death is nothing more than separation. Physical death is the separation of your spirit and soul from your physical body. There is a worse death. Spiritual death means being separated from God. When Adam chose to believe Satan's word instead of God, man's spirit disconnected from God and fell under the control and authority of Satan. Jesus came to remove the sin of Adam so the original link could be reestablished. When a person accepts Jesus Christ as their savior, a type of re-birth takes place. The spirit man is regenerated. That is why it is called being 'born again'. The Holy Spirit, the third person of the Godhead, actually comes to indwell the believer. The Holy Spirit enables the human spirit to again communicate with God. Only a spirit can communicate with another spirit. God is spirit and so man can only communicate with Him through his human spirit. The Holy Spirit is the link. That's why John recorded the following words of Jesus:

Yet a time is coming and has now come when the true worshipers will worship the Father in spirit and truth, for they are the kind of worshipers the Father seeks. God is Spirit and his worshipers must worship in spirit and in truth.

John 4:23-24

"In spirit and in truth." What is truth? Truth is whatever comes out of the mouth of God. Worshipping in truth means coming into agreement with what God says. Truth is not arbitrary. There can only be one truth. Bless God, He did not keep it a secret from us. He did not hide it on top of a mountain somewhere forcing you to go on some magical quest to find it. In fact, He has gone out of His way to reveal His truth to mankind. He caused His written Word to be recorded so it could be easily read. Then He sent His Son to confirm it and explain it. If that were not enough, He sent the Holy Spirit to illuminate minds and give understanding to those who seek it. Man is truly without excuse if he does not find it.

Man must be viewed as a whole to understand the principles of healing. Sin caused spiritual death and physical deterioration and death. You must understand one thing. God does not cause bad things to happen. Bad things happen because of the sin problem in this world. Sin is **THE** problem. God had given man authority over this earth. Adam's sin relinquished that authority to Satan. The sin problem manifests in three ways:

- Living in a sin-fallen world
(sickness, disease, natural disasters, rape, murder, etc.)
- Consequences of your own sin
(sickness, sexual disease, injury, divorce, etc.)
- Direct attacks of Satan
(sickness, disease, injury, temptation, curses, witchcraft, death)

Because sin caused both physical and spiritual destruction, BOTH must be delivered in order to achieve and maintain health and healing. Let's look at all three components and their role in achieving healing.

Spirit The center of faith. Head knowledge must become heart (spirit) knowledge and faith explodes!

Soul mind, will, emotions, personality
(center of the intellect)
The soul must understand and believe healing is available and it is God's will to heal.

Body Physical manifestation of healing is achieved.
Knowledge + Faith = Healing

Since knowledge is a key component, we will begin by looking at several aspects of knowledge.

KNOWLEDGE

CHAPTER TWO

KNOWLEDGE OF SALVATION

God, Himself, gives the reason His people are perishing.

My people are destroyed from lack of knowledge.
Hosea 4:6

Knowledge of what? Knowledge of the truth of God's Word. Remember, Jesus said we must worship Him in Spirit and **truth**. Truth is whatever comes out of the mouth of God. He didn't hide it from us either. He made certain it was written down. God's word is the Bible and it is available for us to read.

My son, pay attention to what I say; listen closely to my words. Do not let them out of your sight, keep them within your heart; for they are life to those who find them and health to a man's whole body.
Proverbs 4:20-22

It is absolutely essential to learn what God's word says and to obey it. That brings us to our first order of business. God's primary command is that we accept His Son, Jesus, as

21

our personal savior. It is the only way to achieve salvation and regenerate your spirit man.

Jesus answered, "I am the way and the truth and the life. No one comes to the Father except through me.

John 14:6

God's word tells us that because of the sin of Adam, we are all guilty. We are all sinners in need of a savior. God knew man would sin and He completed a plan before He created the world. Sin was not a surprise to God. It was an outgrowth of man's free-will choice. God gave man a free will so He could have true fellowship with him. He didn't create robots in forced obedience. He wanted man to choose to obey out of love for Him.

Adam's sin caused man to be taken prisoner by Satan. When Adam chose to believe Satan's word instead of God's Word, he placed himself under Satan's authority. Because man introduced sin into the world, man would have to get rid of it. So God, Himself, took the form of a man by being born of a woman. His lineage goes all the way back to Adam. He was a legal representative of man. In contrast to Adam, He came to live a sinless life, reveal the Word of God, the character of God, and the power of God. Finally, He voluntarily took the entire sin debt of the world upon Himself. Then He gave His life to pay the ransom and redeem man from his captivity.

As He hung on the cross He said, "It is finished." The phrase He actually used was a term used in reference to payment of a debt. It was a term they stamped onto legal documents during that time. It is like our modern-day term, "Paid in Full." Jesus said, "Paid in full."

Adam's sin placed us in allegiance to Satan. Jesus victory over sin gave us a new freedom of choice. Now there are two sides: Jesus or Satan. You can choose a new allegiance. But each person must choose for themselves. How? Believe it and speak it.

If you confess with your mouth, "Jesus is Lord," and believe in your heart that God raised him from the dead, you will be saved. For it is with your heart that you believe and are justified, and it is with your mouth that you confess and are saved.

Romans 10:9-10

If you have never chosen sides, I encourage you to do so now. There is a prayer to help you in the back of this book.

Does God Heal Non-Believers?

Yes, God can, and often does, heal non-believers. This is what we refer to as a healing miracle. It takes no faith on the part of the receiver. It comes by the supernatural, anointing power of God through another individual whom God has empowered. God will use the gift of physical healing for the purpose of bringing people to a saving knowledge of Jesus Christ.

A healing miracle is a wonderful act of grace on God's part. However, you are still left with two problems.

1. You could be waiting for the rest of your life for a healing miracle to manifest.
2. If you are healed and do not accept Jesus as your savior, you will not be able to maintain your healing because Satan will still have legal license in your life.

If you have accepted Jesus as your Lord and Savior, you do not have to be dependent upon miracle workers. You can make your own miracles. The believer is empowered with the Holy Spirit and with faith.

CHAPTER THREE

KNOWLEDGE OF
THE HOLY SPIRIT

What a privilege it is to be a believer in Jesus Christ. What a source of power! Scripture says each believer receives the Holy Spirit.

Now it is God who makes both us and you stand firm in Christ. He anointed us, set his seal of ownership on us, and put his Spirit in our hearts as a deposit, guaranteeing what is to come.

2 Corinthians 1:21-22

God actually sends an exact replica of Jesus to come and indwell your very being. The Holy Spirit is like a mark. He is the sign of your covenant relationship with God through Jesus. This was a blood covenant which is the most binding of all covenants. It cannot be broken. You are marked as a child of God. This mark is the future guarantee of eternal life with God. But that is not the only benefit. The Holy Spirit guarantees our inheritance.

And you also were included in Christ when you heard the word of truth, the gospel of your salvation. Having believed, you were marked in him with a seal, the promised Holy Spirit, who is a deposit guaranteeing our inheritance until the redemption of those who are God's possession--to the praise of his glory.

Ephesians 1:13-14

What inheritance? The inheritance we received when Jesus died. It is all the promises in scripture that belong to God's covenant children. Healing is part of that inheritance.

And if the Spirit of him who raised Jesus from the dead is living in you, he who raised Christ from the dead will also give life to your mortal bodies through his Spirit, who lives in you.

Romans 8:11

The Holy Spirit carries the anointing power of God. He is the same Spirit that raised Jesus from the dead. That's awesome power! This says the Spirit will also give life to our **mortal** bodies. It is our regenerated spirit man who is now able to hook up with the anointing power of God through the Holy Spirit who lives in us. Like Creflo Dollar says, "It's God's SUPER on your NATURAL."

CHAPTER FOUR

KNOWLEDGE OF
THE ENEMY

We have a very real enemy and he's trying to destroy us. Let's start placing the blame where the blame belongs.

Be self-controlled and alert. Your enemy the devil prowls around like a roaring lion looking for someone to devour. Resist him, standing firm in the faith.

1 Peter 5:8-9

No matter whether it's your own sin, the result of living in a sin-fallen world, or a direct attack of the enemy, Satan is behind it all. It is important to realize Satan's tactics. Do yourself a favor. Go through the bible and gather intelligence information on your enemy. When our military prepares for war, they first send spies to gather information about the enemies' strengths, weakness, and tactics. Football teams study films of their opponents' prior games in attempt to learn their strategies. Well, this is more important than a football game. What you learn about the enemy can save your life. Jesus said this of the enemy:

He was a murderer from the beginning, not holding to the truth, for there is no truth in him. When he lies, he speaks his native language, for he is a liar and the father of lies.

John 8:44

Deception is his game. It began in the garden when he assured Eve she would not surely die if she ate of the "tree of the knowledge of good and evil." His deceptions are even more sophisticated today because he has spent thousands of years gathering intelligence information on man. I want you to be aware of his primary deceptions.

Deception #1 – Sickness Comes From God

The enemy has deceived many of us, including preachers and teachers, about the origin of sickness and disease. He has twisted God's Word about testing and trial which has nothing to do with sickness and disease. He has led us to believe God places these things on us to teach us something. That's ridiculous! I remember reading an article in the newspaper about a woman who scalded her five-year-old child to death in a bathtub of hot water. When questioned, she said she was trying to teach him a lesson because he wouldn't stop wetting the bed. The community was outraged. How could a mother use such extreme measures to teach anything? Yet, we accuse God of these same crimes against humanity every day. If God did half the things we accuse him of, He would be in jail right along with that woman.

Jesus said:

The thief comes only to steal and kill and destroy; I have come that they may have life, and have it to the full.

John 10:10

This is truth! Jesus is the healer. Satan is the destroyer. Get it straight and keep it straight. You'd be wise to draw a vertical line right down through the middle of this scripture in your Bible. If Satan can get you to believe your sickness came from God, you will not resist it. You will passively sit by and allow it in your life. It's a lie. Don't buy into it. Jesus also told us a kingdom divided against itself cannot stand. If God put that sickness on you, then changed his mind and decided to heal you, that would be a kingdom divided. It doesn't even make good sense.

Deception #2 – Healing is Not God's Will

We have already seen in John 10:10 that Jesus came to give us life to the full. The Greek word translated 'full' means more than enough, abundantly, overflowing. Well, you certainly can't have abundant life if you're sick, can you?

I pray that you may enjoy good health and that all may go well with you, even as your soul is getting along well.

3 John 1:2

It is God's will to keep us both spiritually and physically healthy. A sick and dying and defeated church is not a good witness to the world. God wants believers who will walk in faith and demonstrate His power to overcome the world. If you truly believe it may be God's will for you to be sick, why are you trying so hard to get well? Shame on you for seeing the doctor.

Healing has always been part of God's provision for His people. Read about the exodus of God's people from slavery in Egypt. God told them to kill a lamb, seal the doorway of their house with its blood, then roast it and eat it. The angel of death would see the blood and pass by. The plague was so destructive that Pharaoh called Moses during the night and told them to get out. The Egyptians even gave them their gold and silver to take with them. They left in the middle of the night and there is no mention of carrying any sick among them. How did that happen? These people were not only slaves, they were being mistreated. Surely there must have been some who were sick, or injured from beatings, or old and dying. Yet there were none. In fact the King James says in Psalm 105:37, *"He brought them forth also with silver and gold: and there was not one feeble person among their tribes."*

How did this miracle happen? Well it must have occurred when they ate the lamb. You see, their salvation included their physical rejuvenation. The exodus is a picture of what Messiah would come to do in the future. Salvation includes complete wholeness: spirit, soul (mind), and body. That is why God also made provision for healing of his people under the Old Covenant. As long as the people were obedient to God's Word, sickness was removed from them. Healing has always been part of the Covenant. The Bible says, of Jesus:

"He is the express image of God."

Hebrews 1:3

This means Jesus perfectly represented the Father in everything He did. Jesus never put sickness on anyone. There is not a single instance in the Gospels where Jesus refused to heal someone. It is abundantly clear, healing is always God's will.

Deception #3 – Healing Is Not Available Today

In the Old Testament (Covenant), God selected a covenant people who would bear His name. It was the nation of Israel. They became His special people and were to be marked by prosperity, health, and success. Sickness and disease came only through their disobedience to the law. God also made provision for their healing through repentance and forgiveness.

He sent forth his word and healed them.

Psalm 107:20

It has always been, and always will be, the **Word** of the Lord which provides healing. Jesus is the **Word** made flesh.

In the beginning was the Word, and the Word was with God, and the Word was God. He was with God in the beginning.

John 1:1-2

The Word became flesh and made his dwelling among us.

John 1:14

Jesus came to bring us the good news! He had come to put an end to the consequences of sin in the world. On one Sabbath, Jesus went to the synagogue and the scroll of Isaiah was given to Him to read. He unrolled it to the verses which prophesied about Him and read:

> *"The Spirit of the Lord is on me, because he has anointed me to preach good news to the poor. He has sent me to proclaim freedom for the prisoners and recovery of sight to the blind, to release the oppressed, to proclaim the year of the Lord's favor." Then he rolled up the scroll, gave it back to the attendant and sat down. The eyes of everyone in the synagogue were fastened on him, and he began by saying to them, "Today this scripture is fulfilled in your hearing."*
>
> Luke 4:18-20

Jesus came to set captives free. This is His work and mission. If Jesus is alive today, and we know He is, then this mission is ongoing. It did not cease.

Satan has tried to convince us that healing died out with the last apostle. Scripture itself contradicts that notion. James was the last apostle and look at how he commissioned the church:

> *Is any one of you sick? He should call the elders of the church to pray over him and anoint him with oil in the name of the Lord. And the prayer offered in faith will make the sick person well; the Lord will raise him up. If he has sinned, he will be forgiven.*
>
> James 5:14-15

James says there shouldn't be any sick among you because the Lord has provided healing under the New Covenant. He says, 'use your faith and get them healed.'

Nothing in scripture implies you must get sick to die. The new covenant provides a life of abundance in Jesus. When the Lord calls your spirit home, you should simply close your eyes and leave your physical body. It should be God's timing. He never intended for you to be evicted from your physical body. Job says,

You will come to the grave in full vigor, like sheaves gathered in season.

Job 5:26

Scripture says:

Jesus Christ is the same yesterday and today and forever.

Hebrews 13:8

If that is true, then Jesus still heals today. He hasn't changed. His mission and ministry are still the same. Healing has not fallen by the wayside. The day of healing is not over, it is TODAY!

Deception #4 – Sin Won't Hurt You

This is still the oldest trick in the book. It worked on Eve and it's still working in the world. Sin gives Satan legal license to wreak havoc in our lives. Don't be fooled. If you have unconfessed sin your life, it is a legal doorway for Satan to bring the curse of sin into your life. Get rid of it. Ask the Holy Spirit to reveal hidden problems to you. Sometimes sin can be subtle. Yet, its consequences are the same. For example, Satan uses the power of offense to trap you. We have opportunities to be offended by others every day. If you <u>allow</u>

yourself to be offended, you will not walk in victory. If you are in strife with anyone, if you harbor hatred, anger, or bitterness in your heart, it is sin. You must deal with it, or it will destroy your health like a cancer. When the Spirit reveals sin, go immediately before the Lord. Repent of those things and ask for forgiveness. Jesus said:

I tell you the truth, if anyone says to this mountain, "Go, throw yourself into the sea," and does not doubt in his heart but believes that what he says will happen, it will be done for him. Therefore, I tell you, whatever you ask for in prayer, believe that you have received it, and it will be yours. And when you stand praying, if you hold anything against anyone, forgive him, so that your Father in heaven may forgive you your sins.

Mark 11:23-25

Jesus says, when you stand speaking to that problem, FORGIVE. This command appears in the same verses where Jesus speaks of exercising your faith. Faith will not work in the midst of an unforgiving heart. Sin in the life of a believer is a breach of contract. It's a break in covenant. You cannot stand on the covenant promises when you're in breach of contract.

If we confess our sins, he is faithful and just and will forgive us our sins and purify us from all unrighteousness.

1 John 1:9

Sin, blocks the anointing power of God. If your breakthrough keeps eluding you, check this area of your life carefully. Repentance restores your relationship with God. God is faithful to forgive which allows the anointing power of God to flow back into your life. It is imperative that we walk in love toward everyone. The number one reason people fail to receive their healing is because of a direct violation of the principle of love. Love is the power source behind the entire covenant. From the creation of man to Jesus' death on the cross, love was the reason.

"For God so loved the world that he gave his one and only son"

John 3:16

Remember, love is the force that drives the covenant.

Deception #5 – You Have No Power Against Evil

Sometimes personal sin is not the problem. Living in a sin-fallen world creates problems of catastrophic proportions. Rape, murder, theft, and all other crimes are the consequence of original sin. Earthquakes, tornadoes, famine, flood, and natural disasters of all kinds also fall into this category. Oftentimes we feel powerless against these forces. However, if we are walking closely with the Lord, He assures us of His protection in all things.

If you make the Most High your dwelling – even the LORD, who is my refuge – no disaster will come near your tent.

Psalm 91:9-10

Making the Lord your dwelling means continually abiding in close fellowship with Him. Where the presence of the Lord is, so is the anointing. The anointing is the burden removing, yoke destroying power of God. Sometimes Satan, himself, puts us under direct attack and tries to harm us. Can we withstand such an attack?

You, dear children, are from God and have overcome them, because the one who is in you is greater than the one who is in the world.

1 John 4:4

Jesus has given us the authority to use His Name on the enemy and command him to leave. Stand against him. Tell him you are a blood bought child of God and he has no right or authority to keep this problem on you. You're not going to accept it. Command him in the Name of Jesus to take whatever he's brought upon you and go! The Spirit of God lives in you and He is more powerful than the enemy.

Revelation 12:11 also tells us we overcome by the **blood** of the lamb and the **word** of our testimony. Plead the blood of Jesus and draw a blood line. Say and keep saying, "In the Name of Jesus, I plead the blood of Jesus. I draw a blood line around myself that the enemy cannot cross." There is power in the blood of Jesus. There is power in the Name of Jesus. There is power in the Word of God. The Spirit who lives in you has the authority to exercise all your rights in the covenant.

FAITH

CHAPTER FIVE

FAITH

The next key ingredient is Faith. Remember the concept:

Knowledge plus Faith = Healing.

Faith is the hookup between your Spirit and God's anointing. Faith is not something you have to pray for. Faith is something you already have. You may have to develop it, but you already have it. You could not have received your salvation if God had not already given you faith.

For it is by grace you have been saved, through faith— and not from yourselves, it is the gift of God.

Ephesians 2:8

For by the grace given me I say to every one of you: Do not think of yourself more highly than you ought, but rather think of yourself with sober judgment, in accordance with the measure of faith God has given you.

Romans 12:3

Paul wrote this to believers. This 'measure of faith' is the same for every believer. God gave it to each of us in equal measure. It is the mustard seed Jesus spoke of in Matthew's gospel.

He told them another parable: "The kingdom of heaven is like a mustard seed, which a man took and planted in his field. Though it is the smallest of all your seeds, yet when it grows, it is the largest of garden plants and becomes a tree, so that the birds of the air come and perch in its branches."

Matthew 13:31-32

You don't need to ask for faith. You already have it. It's what you do with it after you get it that counts. Our struggle is getting it from the seed stage to the tree stage. You are responsible for this part. How? Basically two ways. The first is nourishment.

Consequently, faith comes from hearing the message, and the message is heard through the word of Christ.

Romans 10:17

God's Word is nourishment for the seed. The more of the Word you can get into your spirit, the more your faith will increase. Read all you can about faith and healing in God's word. Listen to tapes. Start speaking it out of your own mouth so your ears can hear you say it. Keep it coming in continually. Eventually it will drop from your intellect (soul) to your heart (spirit). That's when things start happening. God's Word in your spirit starts to produce what the bible calls HOPE. The bible definition of hope is not a 'wish'. It is an earnest expectation of something.

Now faith is being sure of what we hope for and certain of what we do not see.

Hebrews 11:1

The Word actually starts to produce an image of something on the inside of you. So if you mediate on healing scriptures you will begin to start seeing yourself well and healed.

The second condition is to start exercising your faith. If it's just developing, don't try to start at the top, you'll get discouraged. Start where you are. Today you may have enough faith to get you through an operation. But in several years, you may have faith for healing without the operation. Remember faith acts. When you exercise your faith, try to do something you couldn't do before. Get out of bed. If you can't move, try to wiggle your toes. Act on what you believe.

I was just learning about faith when Satan tried a strategic attack against me. (Don't be surprised by this. The enemy will try to steal any revelation of faith you get.) A few weeks before Christmas 1999, I started having trouble with my bottom front teeth. At first it was sensitive to chew food. So I started confessing God's Word about healing over it. During the week, it continued to get worse, but I just kept confessing God's Word. I rebuked the enemy's authority over me. I commanded Satan to take his hands off me and leave.

After a week, I awoke in pain with a large, swollen, white pocket in the gum line. I went to the Lord in prayer and asked whether I should go to the dentist. I had been learning about rebuking things by name and I wasn't' sure what this was. The Lord told me I could go and find out what it was but He didn't want me to do anything else until I came back to Him in prayer. I agreed. I made the appointment and continued confessing God's healing scriptures all morning.

When I arrived at the dentist, the technician took one look and ordered x-rays. As I waited for the x-rays to be developed, a feeling of praise came over me. So, I just started to praise the Lord for my healing. I thanked him for the good report I was going to receive. The dentist came in and started gently poking the area. He apologized, telling me he knew how much it must hurt. That's when I realized it didn't hurt anymore. I said, "No, it doesn't hurt, I believe it's healed." He started laughing, pulled the instrument out of my mouth, and said, "Oh ya, that usually happens when people come to the dentist." As a joke he slapped me on the forehead with the palm of his hand and said, "You're heeeeeld." The poor guy didn't even realize he came into perfect agreement with me. I said, "Yes, I know I am." Well, he didn't believe me and went back to poking around. Though I knew I was healed, the outward manifestation obviously wasn't visible yet. He told me I had an abscess. He instructed me to start a prescription right away. It was Wednesday, and he said I would start feeling better by Saturday. I told him I didn't need it because I was already healed. Of course he didn't believe me and handed me the prescription. Then he started writing another one for pain. I stopped him and said, "No, I really don't need it." He looked at me curiously and said, "Are you sure?" I affirmed I was sure. Then another amazing thing happened. He said, "there's no charge for today. I'm sorry this happened to you. Merry Christmas!"

Let me tell you, I walked out praising the Lord for His faithfulness. Then I acted on it. I never did fill that prescription. I still have it in my prayer journal as a reminder of what faith will do. Within one hour all the visible signs subsided and it never came back. Glory to God! Start where you can. Go to the Lord in prayer and follow His leading. As you begin to see success in small things, it increases your faith for larger things. I have received my healing for many other things, including endometriosis. It will be difficult to believe for healing of cancer when you haven't learned to believe for a headache. It's possible but it will mean isolating yourself from all doubt and unbelief and inundating yourself with God's Word. The point is, get prepared!

Don't trust your feelings. The scripture tells us to walk by faith and not by sight (2 Corinthians 5:7). That also means not by feelings. It took over a week of confessing the Word for it to convince me I was healed. The symptoms were still present as I sat in the dentist's chair praising God for my healing.

From a human perspective, Abraham knew he and Sarah were beyond the child-bearing years. However, his faith in God's Word was stronger than what he saw, or felt.

Yet he did not waver through unbelief regarding the promise of God, but was strengthened in his faith and gave glory to God, being fully persuaded that God had power to do what he had promised.

Romans 4:20-21

He strengthened his faith by meditating on what God said. This says Abraham was fully persuaded. Faith is of no value if placed on something false or unreliable. Place your faith in God's Word. God's Word is the only truth. Meditate on it until you are fully persuaded.

Another key issue in exercising your faith is speaking it out of your mouth. Our words have power. God spoke the universe into existence. We were created in God's image and likeness. Faith-filled words go forth to accomplish their purpose.

Let's look at what Mark wrote again. This time in the King James Version which is a closer translation to the original Greek text.

For verily I say unto you, that whosoever shall say unto this mountain, be thou removed, and be thou cast into the sea; and shall not doubt in his heart, but shall believe that those things which he saith shall come to pass; he shall have whatsoever he saith.

Mark 11:23

For verily (truly) I say (lego). This is a verb meaning to speak forth in words. Whosoever shall say (epo). This is also a verb. It means to speak, in past tense. It happens before the mountain is removed. Believe those things which he saith (lego). He shall have what he saith (lego).

We could put it this way: Whosoever shall speak forth, and shall believe in his heart what he has spoken forth, shall have what he speaks forth. As we meditate on God's Word, it builds an image on the inside of us. Then, when we speak it forth, it becomes reality. It becomes the double-edged sword.

One edge is God's spoken Word. The other edge is that Word, spoken out of your mouth.

The word 'believe,' is the Greek word pisteuo. It means to have confidence in, to put trust in. What is it you are supposed to be trusting? Not your words – God's Word – which can never fail. God said:

So is my word that goes out from my mouth: It will not return to me empty, but will accomplish what I desire and achieve the purpose for which I sent it.

Isaiah 55:11

Jesus said believe, "in your heart" (that's not your head.) Your heart is a reference to your spirit man. How do you believe with your heart? By repetition. Keeping it before your eyes, getting it through your ears and speaking it with your mouth. You build up the spirit man within you by feeding it on God's Word.

In Mark's passage about faith, Jesus only used the word 'believe' once. However, He used the word 'say' three times. Therefore, speaking it must be a priority. Let the confession of your mouth match up with the faith in your heart. Even when I was just starting, I grabbed hold of this principle. When I was speaking healing over my gum abscess, I memorized certain scriptures and would quote them out loud throughout the day. I would say, "I walk by faith and not by sight." "Thank you Lord that you are the God that heals me." "I overcome by the blood of the Lamb and the word of my testimony." "He Himself bore my sicknesses and diseases in His body on the tree and by His wounds I am healed." "He was pierced for my transgressions. He was crushed for my sin and all the consequences of my sin.

The punishment that brought me healing was upon Him and by His wounds I am healed."

Faith is a spiritual force you must exercise. Get the Word coming in and get the Word going forth!

MEDICINE

CHAPTER 6

PERSONAL SCRIPTURE CHAIN

The idea of chaining scriptures together in your bible is designed to assist you in getting through many scriptures of the same topic in an efficient fashion. Begin by placing the first healing scripture reference somewhere in the front cover of your bible. Select a highlighter color such as yellow, blue, or pink to mark the subsequent healing references. When you turn to the first reference, highlight that scripture. At the end of the scripture, make a reference in pen or pencil to the next healing scripture. Highlight that verse or verses and make a reference at the end to the next one, and so on. When you have finished you will have a healing chain. By turning to the first one, your references will take you to all the rest.

The following references will take you through the bible in book order so you won't have to back track. However, you can mark and chain them in any order you wish. You may also choose to add others of your own.

The list is presented first. The remainder of the book will give you more insight into each of the scriptures in this list. The Old Testament was written in Hebrew with some Aramaic. The New Testament was written in Greek. The early translators did the best job they could with their level of understanding. It is also difficult to put Hebrew concepts into English words. Revelation knowledge has continued to increase in the earth and will continue until Jesus returns. I encourage you to study these scriptures out for yourself.

This list is not exhaustive. It is designed to develop faith for healing in your spirit. Always pray and ask the Holy Spirit to give you the key to your situation. It is not the same every time. Only the Holy Spirit knows which Word to quicken to you in any given situation. Watch out about, 'claiming this, and doing that.' Doing without faith is folly. You don't throw your medicine away unless you've heard from the Holy Spirit.

God told the Israelites to cross the Red Sea. They heard, they obeyed and they received their miracle. The Egyptians tried to follow, but God didn't tell them to cross, He told them, "Let my people go." Jesus performed His first miracle at the wedding in Cana. Mary told the servants, Whatever He tells you, Do it! That is the key to miracles.

Exodus 15:26
Exodus 23:25-26
Deuteronomy 7:15
Job 33:24-25
Psalm 91
Psalm 103:1-5
Psalm 107:19-20
Psalm 145:13
Proverbs 3:1-2

Proverbs 4:20-27

Proverbs 15:4

Isaiah 53:4-5

Jeremiah 1:12

Jeremiah 30:17

Matthew 8:16-17

Matthew 15:30

Matthew 18:18

Mark 11:23

Mark 16:17-18

Luke 9:2

Luke 13:16

Acts 5:16

Acts 10:38

Romans 4:20-21

Romans 8:11

Romans 10:17

2 Corinthians 5:7

2 Corinthians 10:4-5

Galatians 3:13-14

Ephesians 6:13

Hebrews 10:35

Hebrews 10:38

Hebrews 11:1

James 1:6-8

James 4:7

James 5:14-15

1 Peter 2:24

1 Peter 5:7

Exodus 15:26

He said, "If you listen carefully to the voice of the Lord your God and do what is right in his eyes, if you pay attention to his commands and keep all his decrees, I will not bring on you any of the diseases I brought on the Egyptians, for I am the Lord, who heals you.

This says listen carefully to the <u>voice</u> of the Lord. That is God's word in scripture, or by direct revelation to you, and/ or by the inner voice of the Spirit within you. Next it says, 'Do what it says!' That's not rocket science. Listen and Do.

It goes on to say, "I will not bring." That phrase, along with the second phrase, 'I brought on,' were both translated from the same Hebrew word 'siym.'[1] It can also be translated, 'to appoint or to ordain.' In this context it means "I will not allow, or I will not permit." The Lord is not the destroyer. However, the Lord is sovereign. Satan cannot bring on you anything the Father does not allow. The key here is God's justice. Because man sinned, Satan has certain legal rights in this world. Therefore, if you do or say something which gives Satan legal license to attack you, God will be required by His justice to allow it.

I believe God is telling us, if you pay attention to what I say and do what I say, I will justly be able to deny Satan any legal authority to keep illness on you. I will veto his authority. God confirms this by declaring, "I am the Healer." He cannot be the healer and the destroyer at the same time. Jesus said a "house divided will fall" (Luke 11:17).

---

[1] Brown, Driver, Briggs Hebrew Lexicon, Strongs #H7760

I started getting flu symptoms one day. I just wanted to lay in the bed. But I knew enough to take my Bible with me. I knew I should read through my healing chain. I only made it to this first scripture. After reading it, I paused and asked the Lord, "Have I done something that has allowed this illness to come on me?" Immediately in my spirit I heard, "You judged Don." I countered with, "Lord, I did not. All I said was . . ." We had a little discussion about it and I realized, of course, the Lord was right. I immediately repented and asked forgiveness. Then I said, "Satan, that sin is forgiven and that doorway is closed. You cannot keep this on me. I demand this sickness leave me now, in Jesus Name." Then, I got myself up out of that bed and started making dinner, just like a normal person. Within one hour every symptom had left me and I never did get that flu.

Exodus 23:25-26

Worship the Lord your God, and his blessing will be on your food and water. I will take away sickness from among you, and none will miscarry or be barren in your land. I will give you a full life span.

The word translated 'worship' is a Hebrew word better translated 'serve.' Serving involves worship but it is much more. It means becoming subject to the Lord and obedient to His commands. When you do this, He promises to bless your food. He says, you do your part and I'll do mine. I will bless (consecrate it, make it holy, guard it, protect it).[2] It's guaranteed. You merely have to thank Him for it.

---

[2] Websters International Dictionary, G.&C. Merriam Company, 1899, Pg. 154

In addition, He says, "I will take away sickness from among you." 'Take away' is a poor translation since God did not put sickness on them in the first place. This Hebrew word is better translated 'turn aside.' For example, to divert a river, you block its original course. God actually steps in and forces the curse away from you!

"I will give you a full life span." This literally means, the number of days (you are entitled to) will be fulfilled or accomplished. Psalm 90:10 tells us we have a general lifespan of 70-80 years. The Jews believe the promise is 120 years as stated in Genesis 6:3. Moses was considered the example. They speak this promise whenever they raise their glass. They say, "ad ma'ah v'esrim shanah" (until 120 years). Scripture does not ever say we must get sick to die. When your life is complete, you will die like Moses. When his work was accomplished, he simply fell asleep and God took him home. The bible says he was 120 years old, in perfect health, with perfect eye sight. God wants you to accomplish the work He assigned to you even before you were born. However, you can die prematurely if you give the enemy license in your life. Don't let Satan evict you from your body.

Deuteronomy 7:15

The LORD will keep you free from every disease. He will not inflict on you the horrible diseases you knew in Egypt, but he will inflict them on all who hate you.

Not only does the Lord want to heal us, He wants to keep us free from sickness and disease. The word translated 'inflict' is the same Hebrew word 'siym'[3] we discussed in Exodus 15:26. It can also be translated, 'to appoint or to ordain.' In this context it means "I will not allow, or I will not permit." Egypt represents the slavery of sin and of this world system. God says He will keep us free from the sickness and disease we knew while we were slaves to this world system.

Job 33:24-25

I have found a ransom for him – then his flesh is renewed like a child's; it is restored as in the days of his youth.

The word we have translated 'ransom' is 'kopher'[4] and literally means 'the price of a life.' In the Old Testament if one of your animals killed another man and you were judged to be negligent, you could be killed. However, the law allowed you to be redeemed by paying the redemption price to the dead man's relatives.

The word 'found' is 'matsa'[5] and means to acquire or attain. God found the solution, not man. God says 'I have recovered what was lost in the fall by paying the redemption price for him.' For who? For anyone who would receive it. For anyone who would place their faith in the one who paid the price—Jesus Christ.

Then, his flesh (referring to the whole body) is renewed (rejuvenated). Sometimes healing doesn't manifest immediately. It may need restoration cell by cell. It is restored

---

[3] Brown, Driver, Briggs Hebrew Lexicon, Strongs #H7760
[4] Ibid. H3724
[5] Ibid. H4672

(to return back) to the days of his youth (vigor). These Hebrew verbs are present tense. It does not mean after you die. It is referring to the here and now!

Psalm 91
(Entire Psalm)

You may wish to highlight only the title (Psalm 91) to remind you to read the entire psalm. Then place your next reference at the end of psalm 91. Turn to Psalm 91 now and read it with some of these insights.

91:1 – Dwells is 'yashab'[6] to dwell, settle, abide, remain, inhabit

Shelter is 'sithrah'[7] shelter, secret place, hiding place, covering

Shadow is 'tsel'[8] shadow, defense, protection

91:2 – "I will SAY of the Lord" means speak, boast, tell

You need to speak this out of your own mouth.

91:4 – "He will cover you with his feathers"

I remember a story Malcolm Smith told about visiting a barnyard after a terrible fire. He saw a pile of old black rags and kicked them as he walked by. Out from underneath ran a bunch of little yellow chicks. You see it wasn't a pile of old rags. It was the mother hen. She had spread her wings out to cover them and let the fire sweep over her instead. She perished but her children

---

[6] Brown, Driver, Briggs Hebrew Lexicon, Strongs #H3427

[7] Ibid, H5643

[8] Ibid, H6738

were spared. That is what God will do for us. What an awesome God we serve.

91:7 – You can be standing in the middle of a crisis affecting everyone around you, and yet go untouched.

91:9 – "If you make the Most High your dwelling" (refuge) How? Verse 2, SAY and TRUST.

91:11 – Believers are assigned angels whom we can call on for defense. Angels respond to the Word of God. You must quote the Word. Then dispatch them to do what the Word says.

91:16 – The full number of your intended days and more if you are not satisfied. God wants you to be satisfied.

Psalm 103:1-5

Praise the Lord, O my soul; all my inmost being, praise his holy name. Praise the Lord, O my soul, and forget not all his benefits – who forgives all your sins and heals all your diseases, who redeems your life from the pit and crowns you with love and compassion, who satisfies your desires with good things so that your youth is renewed like the eagle's.

The word 'praise' is 'barak'[9] also translated 'bless.' It means to kneel as an act of adoration. This says glorify the Lord from the heart: from your inner man. That is more than lip service. It's an appreciation of who God is. It says, 'glorify his Name.' God's Name is who He is. He is love. He is faithfulness. He is mercy. He doesn't just <u>have</u> these things. He <u>is</u> these things. As your inner man gets revelation knowledge of

---

[9] Brown, Driver, Briggs Hebrew Lexicon, Strongs #H1288

who God is, that knowledge enlarges your capacity to receive from Him. Notice that the same anointing to forgive sins, also heals. It's all part of the redemption. Keep all the benefits in mind: salvation, healing, removal of the curse, His pledge of love to you, restoration of the blessing, and a renewing of your very life.

You cannot get revelation knowledge of who God is without staying in His Word, studying it, and meditating on it. It is possible to get so much of God's Word into you, that your physical body will be blessed by default. Even your youthful vigor will be restored by this knowledge in your inner man.

Psalm 107:19-20

Then they cried to the Lord in their trouble, and he saved them from their distress. He sent forth his word and healed them.

'Cried' is 'zaaq'[10] and literally means to shriek: to call out from anguish. It's an SOS call for help. The word 'trouble' 'mᵉtsuqah'[11] means a narrow or tight place, distress, or an adversary, opponent, or oppressor.

He 'saved' is the Hebrew word 'yasha'[12] which means to be delivered, set free, rescued, or liberated. It also means to be victorious in battle.

How does the Lord deliver? He 'sent forth' His Word also means 'to let loose.' What does He let loose? His Word.

---

[10] Brown, Driver, Briggs Hebrew Lexicon, Strongs #H2199
[11] Ibid. H4691
[12] Ibid. H3467

The implication of this Hebrew word is that of a legal decree. God's Word stands. It cannot be disputed.

His Word is loosed to 'heal' them. Heal is the Hebrew word 'rapha'[13]. It implies mending, as water is to pottery. It is the word for healing, physician, cure, repair, and to make whole.

God wants you restored to health: spirit, soul (mind), and body. All broken parts mended. He wants you whole!

Psalm 145:13

The Lord is faithful to all his promises[14]

God is Faithful. God is Truth. God cannot lie. When you find a promise of God in the bible, you can depend on it. Meditate on God's faithfulness. Praise Him for it.

Proverbs 3:1-2

My son, do not forget my teaching, but keep my commands in your heart, for they will prolong your life many years and bring you prosperity.

'Do not forget.' That is to stop caring about, ignore, or stop giving attention to. Keep my commands (laws, instructions, teachings) in your heart. Again we see reference to our inner man. The Word gets into our inner man by meditating

---

[13] Brown, Driver, Briggs Hebrew Lexicon, Strongs #H7495

[14] *Note: The last two lines of verse 13 do not appear in most manuscripts of the Masoretic text and as such may not appear in your King James Version. It does appear in one version of the Masoretic text as well as the Dead Sea Scrolls and Syriac.

on it day and night. Keep it coming into your eyes and ears. Keep it coming out of your mouth.

For they (God's instructions) will prolong (add, increase, lengthen) your life and bring you shalom. The Hebrew word 'shalom'[15] is difficult to define in English. We have no corresponding English equivalent because it's not really a word, it's a concept. We translate it 'peace' but it means much more than that. It comes from a root word meaning 'wholeness.' Therefore, it means the peace that comes from being whole. It means peace, prosperity, health, safety, protection, tranquillity, peace of mind – a general wholeness and well being. God's Word can make you whole – nothing missing, nothing broken.

Proverbs 4:20-27

My son, pay attention to my words. Do not let them out of your sight, keep them within your heart, for they are life to those who find them and health to a man's whole body. Above all else, guard your heart, for it is the wellspring of life. Put away perversity from your mouth; keep corrupt talk far from your lips. Let your eyes look straight ahead, fix your gaze directly before you. Make level paths for your feet and take only ways that are firm. Do not swerve to the right or the left; keep your foot from evil.

---

[15] Brown, Driver, Briggs Hebrew Lexicon, Strongs #H7965

The word 'keep' is 'shamar.'[16] It is a root word meaning to hedge about. It means guard the Word, preserve it, treasure it up in memory. The emphasis is on repetition and memorization. Do not let God's Word be stolen from you.

The Hebrew word translated 'health' 'marpe'[17] to a man's whole body is also translated 'remedy' or 'cure.' Taking in God's Word daily is like medicine. Use it as you would use physical medicine. Oftentimes medicine is prescribed as a prophylactic, such as an aspirin a day to prevent heart disease. That means taking it before you get sick in order to prevent a problem. That's the best way to take God's medicine.

'Guard your heart' – The idea is to be diligent about this, like a watchman. Stay away from doubt and unbelief. It may mean disassociating from certain people, places, things, music, movies, etc. When you hear negative words, simply say, "I don't receive that" and put it out of your mind. Quote God's Word instead.

A 'wellspring' is the source of a spring or stream. Your 'heart' or inner spirit man is the 'wellspring of life.' Out of it flow the forces of life. Healing does not come on you. It is a spiritual force flowing from inside your heart (spirit).

'Put away 'perversity.' This word is 'iqqshuwth'[18] and comes from a root word meaning crooked, twisted, or distorted. It specifically refers to speech. If something does not line up with God's Word, it is false. Do not speak words contradictory to the Word of God. It says remove negative speech far (a great distance) from you. Even while experiencing symptoms and

---

[16] Brown, Driver, Briggs Hebrew Lexicon, Strongs #H8104
[17] Ibid. H4832
[18] Ibid. H6143

someone asks how you're doing, say, "Bless God, these symptoms can't stay on me. God's Word says I'm healed."

'Fix your gaze' means to look intently: straight at the goal.

'Make level paths' means clear the way of any obstacles to your faith. Don't deviate. Don't take your focus off God and His Word. Look straight ahead. Stay on the path.

Proverbs 15:4

The tongue that brings healing is a tree of life, but a deceitful tongue crushes the spirit.

Whole books can be written on the power of your words. God spoke everything into being. We are made in the image and likeness of God. As a born-again believer, you become a son or daughter of the living God. Your words have power. God intended for you to use them for good. Jesus defeated sin, sickness, disease, poverty, lack, and every evil thing on the cross. However, if you choose to speak words in opposition to God's word, it gives Satan legal license to carry out what you speak.

For example: I've heard men say, "I'll probably die of a heart attack because my father and grandfather both did." They do not realize they have just come into agreement with the problem. A spiritual law comes into play giving Satan license to exercise the power of those words. Don't speak the problem, speak the solution.

"A tongue that brings healing" is better translated, "a healing or curative tongue." A tree portrays the idea of being firmly established. God says you can use the curative power in your tongue to bring (firmly established) life.

"But a deceitful tongue," the word 'deceitful' is 'celeph'[19] and means distorted, vicious, crooked or perverse. Crooked implies a path away from God. A distortion is anything in opposition to God's Word.

"Crushes the spirit" is not a good translation. The Hebrew word 'sheber'[20] actually means a breach or fracture. It (a distorted tongue) causes a breach or fracture in the spirit. The Hebrew word used for spirit is 'ruach'[21] and also means breath. God's breath within you implies life. In other words, your spirit or 'heart' has been breached by your own words.[22] In warfare a breach in the wall allows the enemy to penetrate. Do not underestimate the power of your words. Speak only faith. That old saying our mothers taught us is actually true. "If you don't have anything good to say, don't say anything at all."

Isaiah 53:4-5

Surely he took up our infirmities and carried our sorrows, yet we considered him stricken by God, smitten by him, and afflicted. But he was pierced for our transgressions, he was crushed for our iniquities; the punishment that brought us peace was upon him, and by his wounds we are healed.

---

[19] Brown, Driver, Briggs Hebrew Lexicon, Strongs #H5558

[20] Ibid. H7667

[21] Ibid. H7307

[22] For further information, I recommend a tape, Power of the Tongue, by Kenneth Copeland. Contact Kenneth Copeland Ministries Fort Worth, Texas.

This is one of my favorite scriptures. It is the heart of the work Jesus came to achieve on the cross.

'Infirmities' is the Hebrew word 'choliy'[23] and means sickness, disease, grief, weakness, anxiety, and/or calamity.

'Sorrows' is 'mak'ob'[24] meaning anguish, affliction—sorrow, pain, grief. It comes from a root word meaning to have pain or to be made sad, sore, or grieving. It implies both physical and emotional pain.

Isaiah prophesied that Messiah (Jesus) would take upon Himself all these negative results of the curse. They were judged by God at the cross who allowed the full punishment of Adam's sin to fall upon Jesus. In fact the word translated 'afflicted' is an interesting Hebrew root word that carries the meaning: 'to abase self,' 'answer for,' or 'afflict self.' The God of the universe voluntarily took the punishment for us so that we could be made free. He was pierced for our transgressions (revolt, rebellion). He was crushed (bruised, broken) for our iniquity.

The word 'iniquity' is 'avon'[25] and it means sin and all the consequences of sin. Guess what the consequences of sin are. Pain, sickness, disease, poverty, lack, fear, and every bad thing the enemy throws at us. Jesus died to redeem us from our sin as well as all the consequences of our sin.

"The punishment that brought us peace was upon him." Remember the Hebrew word translated 'peace' is 'shalom' and means wholeness: health, prosperity, safety, protection, well

---

[23] Brown, Driver, Briggs Hebrew Lexicon, Strongs #H2483

[24] Ibid. H4341

[25] Ibid. H5771

being in mind and body. The punishment Jesus took brought us total deliverance from the effects of the curse.

"By His wounds we <u>are</u> (rapha) healed!" Not 'gonna be', ARE! It was accomplished 2000 years ago. We ARE cured, mended, repaired. We ARE restored to Shalom. Praise God! You must get a revelation of this. Meditate on it. Stand on it!

This is my confession: Surely, Jesus carried all my pain, emotional and physical. He was pierced because of my rebellion. He was bruised and broken for sin and all the consequences of sin. His punishment bought me peace, health, prosperity, and safety and by His wounds, I AM made whole. Hallelujah!

Jeremiah 1:12

I am watching to see that my word is fulfilled.

The word translated 'watching' is 'shaqad'[26] meaning being alert to, causing it to hasten. In fact it carries the implication of being so watchful that one would loose sleep over it. Although God doesn't worry, it portrays the idea of not allowing Himself to rest until it is accomplished.

'Fulfilled' is the Hebrew word 'asah'[27] also meaning to accomplish, or to execute as in a legal document. It carries the implication of doing work to produce a result.

God is saying He constantly watches every Word He has uttered. He works toward making it produce everything He intended and He enforces its legal authority.

---

[26] Brown, Driver, Briggs Hebrew Lexicon, Strongs #H8245
[27] Ibid. H6213

In fact, the scripture tells us angels harken to the Word of God (Psalm 103:20). When you speak God's Word out of your mouth, angels are immediately dispatched to assist you in achieving results in the Spirit realm.

Jeremiah 30:17

But I will restore you to health and heal your wounds, declares the Lord.

The word translated 'restore' is 'alah'[28]. It is a primitive root word meaning to raise up. It can be used of a new day dawning. It implies drawing something forth, to recover, to spring up, to grow, to shoot forth like a new branch.

'Health' is 'arukah'[29] and means restoring to soundness or wholeness, perfected. Complete health in spirit, soul (mind) and body. The word 'heal' is again 'rapha' meaning to cure as a physician, repair (as a potter), thoroughly make whole.

'Wounds' is 'makkah'[30] and means a wound, a blow, a beating, or a plague. It comes from a word meaning smitten with disease, pestilence, or attacks of an enemy.

'Declares the LORD.' There are different words for God in scripture. The particular word used here was Jehovah. It is a translation of the word Yahweh. It refers to God as the self-existing One who is the one true God. This name is God's personal, covenant name. Our God is a covenant keeping God. God is sovereign and can do as He pleases. However, in His sovereignty He has chosen to bind Himself to His Word and

---

[28] Brown, Driver, Briggs Hebrew Lexicon, Strongs #H5927
[29] Ibid. H724
[30] Ibid. H4347

His covenant promises. Therefore, He is bound to heal when His Word is acted upon.

Matthew 8:16-17

He drove out the spirits with a word and healed all the sick. This was to fulfill what was spoken through the prophet Isaiah: "He took up our infirmities and carried our diseases."

Spirits, in this case, refer to evil spirits (demonic possession.) Jesus drove them out. The New Testament is written in Greek. The Greek word for 'drove' is 'ekballo'[31] and means to forcibly expel, eject or drive out. Jesus used the Word of God to forcibly eject demons which can also be a source of physical or emotional illness.

The words translated 'sick' is a combination of two Greek words "kakos echontas"[32] and literally means 'having badly.' 'Kakos' implies being held bound or gripped. 'Echontas' means sick, diseased, miserable, or wretched. Interestingly enough it carries the implication of occurring improperly or wrongly. This affirms that neither sickness nor disease come from God. It is evil and; therefore, comes from Satan. God does not use Satan as a tool. Satan is strictly self employed. God's people are improperly held bound by sickness and disease. Jesus has the power to break those bonds. Why? The second part tells us. It refers us back to the passage in Isaiah 53:4-5 which you have already studied. Jesus took the

---

[31] Thayer's Greek Lexicon, Strongs #G1544
[32] Ibid. G2556 & G2192

whole curse upon himself and defeated it on Calvary's cross. Glory to God!

Matthew 15:30

Great crowds came to him, bringing the lame, the blind, the crippled, the mute and many others, and laid them at his feet; and he healed them.

Great crowds came and Jesus healed them all. You will find many other references in scripture reiterating, "He healed them all." Jesus did not pick and choose. Scripture says the Lord does not show favoritism (Acts 10:34, Romans 2:10-11). There is no reference in scripture where Jesus refused to heal anyone who came to Him for healing. Why? If, as some people teach, God puts sickness on them to teach them something, why didn't Jesus say to a least one person, "I'm sorry I cannot heal you, the sickness you have is God's will." I'll tell you why. Sickness is NEVER God's will. Jesus proved it by healing them ALL. If Jesus is the same yesterday, today, and forever (Hebrews 13:8), then Jesus heals today just as he did during His ministry on earth.

Matthew 18:18

I tell you the truth, whatever you bind on earth will be bound in heaven, and whatever you loose on earth will be loosed in heaven.

Jesus starts this discourse with "Amen, I say unto you." NIV translates it, "I tell you the truth." Some translations use terms like 'Verily' or 'Most Assuredly.' 'Amen' is a Greek word of Hebrew origin. It comes from the Hebrew root word Aman (believe)[33]. It came to mean 'sure' or 'truly,' an expression of absolute trust and confidence. No matter how it is translated, whenever Jesus said it, He meant, "Pay attention to what I'm going to say next. I'm going to tell you a very important truth."

'Whatever' means as many as, as great as, as long as. No limits.

'Bind' is 'deo'[34] and means tie, fasten, put in chains. It also means forbid, prohibit, or declare to be unlawful.

'Loose' is 'luo'[35] and means break, destroy, dissolve, set free, unbind, untie, release.

It helps me to use the terms disallow and allow in place of bind and loose. When Adam sinned he relinquished his God-given authority over this world to Satan. When Jesus paid the penalty for that sin, there was a transfer of authority to Jesus. See Matthew 28:18. As Jesus' representatives on this earth, He has delegated His authority to us, born-again believers.

Rebuke the enemy. Command him to leave. Command him to take sickness and disease and be gone. Bind him from interfering in your life. Then loose, God's blessings from His Word into your life.

---

[33] Brown, Driver, Briggs Hebrew Lexicon, Strongs#H539, & Thayer's Greek Lexicon, Strongs #G281

[34] Thayer's Greek Lexicon, Strongs #G1210

[35] Ibid. G3089

Mark 11:23

"For verily I say unto you, That whosoever shall say unto this mountain, Be thou removed, and be thou cast into the sea, and shall not doubt in his heart, but shall believe that those things which he saith shall come to pass, he shall have whatsoever he saith" (KJV)[36].

Jesus again says, "Amen" or "I tell you the truth." That means listen carefully, profound truth is coming!

"Whosoever shall say." Are you a whosoever? Of course you are. Can you speak to the problem? Of course you can. The verse goes on to say, "does not doubt in his heart." The word for 'doubt' means to waver or to hesitate. The 'heart' refers to the inner, spirit man. It does not refer to the physical heart nor to the mind. It refers to the spirit. Faith comes forth from the spirit man. It is more than head knowledge. In fact, your head can doubt and it will still work if it comes out of the heart. How do you get it into your heart? The Bible says, faith comes by hearing the Word of God (Romans 10:17). The spirit man responds to the Word of God. Hebrews 11:1 says, Now faith is the substance of things hoped for, the evidence of things not seen. Romans 4:17 tells us to call those things that are not as though they are.

No matter what the circumstance looks like, start speaking God's Word to the situation and don't stop. Faith isn't doing you any good if you're quiet. Faith speaks (Romans 10:8). Faith is released through speaking God's Word out of our mouth. Jesus said, "say" to the mountain. Then He said, believe what you "say." Remember, God spoke the universe

---

36 Scripture taken from the Holy Bible King James Version

into being (Hebrews 11:3). Then Jesus said you shall have what you "say." I don't know why God sovereignly chose to set it up this way, but He did. So get over it. There's power in the spoken word.

Speak these scriptures out loud until they get down into your heart (faith cometh). For example, say, "I am the healed of the Lord. Jesus bore my sickness and disease and by His wounds I am healed now in Jesus Name."

Mark 16:17-18

And these signs will accompany those who believe: In my name they will drive out demons; they will speak in new tongues; they will pick up snakes with their hands; and when they drink deadly poison, it will not hurt them at all; they will place their hands on sick people, and they will get well.

"These signs will accompany those who believe." In other words, faith in the Name of Jesus will cause supernatural things to happen in the life of a believer. One of these 'signs' involves healing. "They will lay hands on sick people, and they will get well." Sometimes people are not yet at the level of faith whereby they can obtain their own healing. Believers are instructed to lay hands on them and believe God with them for their healing. God provides a way for all to be healed. If this is the level of faith you are at, don't be discouraged. Receive your healing this way and continue on in the Word until you are able to lay hands on others. That's what it's all about. Helping one another to grow spiritually and standing in the gap for each other in the meantime.

Stretch your faith out and believe along with another believer for your healing. Start confessing your healing from that point on no matter what the situation looks like. Listen to the voice of the Spirit as you pray and do whatever He tells you to do.

Luke 9:2

. . . and he sent them out to preach the kingdom of God and to heal the sick.

While Jesus was still on earth He sent his twelve apostles on a training mission. He gave them His authority and sent them out to preach the kingdom and heal the sick. What is the kingdom of God? It simply means the rule and reign of God. There are currently two kingdoms in operation: the physical kingdom of this world and God's kingdom. The rules of each kingdom are vastly different. Because God's kingdom represents His reign, the laws and principles of His kingdom supersede all natural laws and principles. Remember that. Spiritual laws supersede natural laws! Sickness and disease is a natural fact. It is a fact caused by the curse. However, God's Word is truth. Therefore, Truth can change any fact controlled by the curse.

He instructed them to preach the kingdom because it's our affiliation with God's kingdom that guarantees our healing. In God's kingdom, shalom rules: peace, prosperity, health, safety, wholeness. The good news of God's Kingdom produces faith. Jesus said, 'Tell them about the kingdom and then heal them all.'

Who is eligible to receive this healing? Whosoever! Whoever will hear and believe. No one is excluded except those who do not believe. God cannot show favoritism. The kingdom laws work for everyone equally because they are exactly that: laws. They are as certain as the natural law of gravity. Jesus sent them out to demonstrate the transfer of authority soon to occur upon His death and resurrection. They did what Jesus told them to do and came back rejoicing because it worked. All believers now have this authority in Jesus Name.

Luke 13:16

Then should not this woman, a daughter of Abraham, whom Satan has kept bound for eighteen long years, be set free . . .?

This is another of my favorites because it is covenant talk: "A daughter of Abraham." You see, God had cut a blood covenant with Abraham (the father of the Hebrew nation). It was to be an everlasting covenant to all of Abraham's descendants. One provision of covenant guarantees the assistance of your covenant partner when under attack by an enemy. Jesus came as representative of the Covenant. He was saying, "Satan has no authority to keep this disease on any child protected by the covenant."

"Whom Satan has kept bound." The word translated 'bound' is, again, 'deo' and means to bind, imprison, or fasten with chains. Jesus clearly said this affliction came from the enemy. The word translated 'set free' is the same word we studied earlier as 'loosed.' Jesus said the enemy is required to release her because she is a child of the covenant promises.

Believers also become children of Abraham. They are grafted into the family (see Galatians 3:7-8). Jesus came and confirmed the covenant of shalom in His own blood. It is a dual adoption. Jesus was both God and man. On man's side we are adopted into the family of Abraham. On God's side, we are adopted into the family of God. But, God maintained our right to choose. Just as a man chose to accept the mark of circumcision in the Abrahamic Covenant, we must choose to accept Jesus, and receive the mark of the Holy Spirit (see Ephesians 1:13-14). When we choose Jesus, we can stand in Jesus' blood, boldly proclaim the covenant rules to Satan and God will enforce it.

Acts 5:16

. . . and all of them were healed.

Notice, again, all were healed. Not some, not a few, not certain cases. All who came were healed. No exceptions. Not one time did Jesus say, "No its God's will that you are bearing this sickness." Not once. The word in town was, 'If you can get to Jesus, you will be healed.' None were disappointed. That truth is the same today. God says He is the same yesterday, today, and forever (Hebrews 13:8).

I said, "If you can get to Jesus." How do you get to Jesus? By inviting Him to come into your heart and proclaiming Him Lord of your life. In that instant, God says you are adopted into the family with all the rights and privileges of Jesus Himself. There is no better deal going than that!

Acts 10:38

How God anointed Jesus of Nazareth with the Holy Spirit and power, and how he went around doing good and healing all who were under the power of the devil, because God was with him.

Most people believe Jesus could heal because He was the Son of God. It is true, He is the Son of God; and it is true that He could have healed because of that fact. However, that is not HOW Jesus healed. This was a great revelation to me. Let's go back and look at Jesus baptism. Matthew 3:13-17 tells us Jesus came to John the Baptist to be baptized. When He came up out of the water, the heavens opened and John saw the Spirit of God descend upon Him as a dove and lightening. The audible voice of God was heard saying,"This is my Son." Luke 3:23 tells us Jesus was about 30 years old when this happened. This is when His public ministry began. He was baptized and anointed with the Holy Spirit. Then Jesus began healing, performing miracles, and casting out demons.

Let me ask you a question. Wasn't Jesus just as much the Son of God at age 16 or 18 or 21? Yet, He did not heal or perform miracles or cast out demons. Wasn't Jesus just as much the Son of God the day before His baptism? Yet He hadn't healed one person, nor performed one miracle, nor cast out one demon. Why? Because He waited for the anointing of the Holy Spirit. Why did He wait? Why didn't He just use His own power as the Son of God? Are you ready for the answer?

The Bible says He is the firstfruits of a new creation (1Corinthians 5:20, James 1:18). He wasn't going to heal any other way than He would empower His followers to heal. He was not going to allow us to sit back 2000 years later and say, "Oh I can't do that. Jesus could only do that because He was the Son of God." That true. He was. But that's not how He did it. He did it by the anointing. The same anointing He promised all believers in His Name. In Luke 3:16, John the Baptist called Jesus the one who would come and baptize with the Holy Spirit. All believers have the same power resident within them that Jesus had. We are able to heal, perform miracles, and cast out demons the same way He did it – under the anointing! Jesus said, "You will receive power when the Holy Spirit comes on you" (Acts 1:8).

Did you notice the last line in this verse: "Because God was with Him." Guess what? Jesus told us the same thing. Then Jesus came to them and said, "All authority in heaven and on earth has been given to me. Therefore, go and make disciples of all nations, baptizing them in the name of the Father and of the Son and of the Holy Spirit, and teaching them to obey everything I have commanded you. And **surely I am with you always,** to the very end of the age" (Matthew 28:18-20, emphasis mine). Don't tell me you can't do it. Jesus says you can. If you have made Jesus Lord of your life and are now positioned 'in Him,' you have the same anointing available to you that Jesus had because He now lives in you permanently. Glory to God!

Romans 4:20-21

Yet he did not waver through unbelief regarding the promise of God, but was strengthened in his faith and gave glory to God, being fully persuaded that God had power to do what he had promised.

The word translated 'waver' is 'diakrino'[37] and means to doubt, dispute, question, withdraw from, or oppose. Paul gives us the reason he was strong in faith and did not waver. He says Abraham was 'fully persuaded.' Becoming fully persuaded only happens one way. Staying, single minded, in God's Word. Stay in the Word. Take the Word like medicine. When the doctor prescribes medicine you usually trust it will work and you take it. Well, take the Word like medicine. Trust it to work. Physical medicine doesn't necessarily work overnight either, but you don't stop taking it. Be fully persuaded. Start praising God for your healing. Start thanking Him for it even before you see it.

Romans 8:11

But if the Spirit of him that raised up Jesus from the dead dwell in you, he that raised up Christ from the dead shall also quicken your mortal bodies by his Spirit that dwelleth in you (KJV)[38]

Jesus promised to send the Holy Spirit to indwell anyone who would receive Him (Jesus) as their personal savior. This is the same Spirit who raised Jesus from the dead. He will

---

[37] Thayer's Greek Lexicon, Strongs #G1252
[38] Scripture taken from the Holy Bible King James Version

quicken our mortal bodies at the second coming of Jesus; but it's also for the here and now. God the Father, by the power of the Holy Spirit, raised up the mortal man, Jesus. Jesus was declared the Messiah, the anointed One (Christ), and made head of the Church. His title 'Christ' designates Him as the source of salvation and our hope of future resurrection.

This same Spirit now indwells each believer. He is able to deliver quickening power to our physical, mortal bodies. The Greek Word 'quicken' is 'zoopoieo'[39] and means: to make alive, to come alive, to give life. You may have heard the term in speaking of a fingernail injury. Someone will say, "Oh, I cut that to the quick." It hurt because it went down into the living part of the nail bed. The Spirit makes alive our mortal bodies.

This is the scripture the Holy Spirit brought to me when I had a severe back injury. I was getting ready to go to the hospital but I didn't want to. I had been standing on the healing scriptures for days but the pain didn't let up. As I was standing there I said, "Lord, I don't know what to do. Please tell me what to do." In my spirit, I heard, "Romans 8:11." This was a scripture I was well acquainted with as I had been meditating upon it for about a month. I knew that if the Holy Spirit gave me a Word, I needed to speak it out of my mouth. So I began to quote Romans 8:11 slowly, considering each word. Then, I quoted it again a second time, considering every word. No change. So I quoted it again a third time. When I finished quoting it the third time, I felt something like electricity hit me on the back of the neck and, like lightening, went all the way

---

[39] Thayer's Greek Lexicon, Strongs #G2227

down my spine. All the pain went with it. I began praising God and dancing around the room, completely healed.

The Holy Spirit can rejuvenate, restore, revive, revitalize, repair, refurbish; and, if necessary, recreate any part of our mortal bodies. Remember, you have to get the Word into your spirit man. The Holy Spirit cannot draw something out of you that you do not have in you. He reaches into your reservoir of scripture stored up in your heart through study, prayer and meditation. But when the Holy Spirit draws on one of those verses in a time of need, the first thing you must do is put it in your mouth, speak it and believe it. Jesus responded to every temptation by Satan in the wilderness with, "It is written." A rhema (revealed) word given at the right time is designed to deliver a fatal blow to the enemy.

Romans 10:17

Consequently, faith comes from hearing the message, and the message is heard through the word of Christ.

How do you increase your faith. By the hearing the Word of Christ. In this passage, it is called the 'Word of Christ' because it refers to the good news of Jesus Christ, which is the foundation for saving faith. His work of salvation includes our physical healing. It is the 'anointed' Word. Keep it before your eyes. Speak it out of your mouth so your ears can hear it. Listen to tapes on healing. Listen to tapes with the healing scriptures pre-recorded for you. Make your own tape and listen to it. Why make your own tape? Because researchers have shown that you will believe yourself faster than you will believe anyone else. No matter how you do it, keep God's Word coming in and going out. The Word WORKS!

2 Corinthians 5:7

We live by faith, not by sight.

Let the eyes of your inner man, your spirit, see what your physical eyes do not yet see. Don't let circumstances force you to take your eyes off Jesus. The truth of God's word will change facts. Remember that. Truth changes facts! God's Word is truth.

Remember when Jairus came to get Jesus because His daughter was dying. Jairus <u>spoke</u> his words of faith. He said, "Please come and put your hands on her so that she will be healed and live." While they were still on their way, some men came from his house and said, 'Its too late, your daughter has just died. Don't bother Jesus anymore.' Jesus, who was speaking to the woman with the issue of blood, cut Himself off in mid sentence, wheeled around, looked Jairus straight in the eye and said, "Don't be afraid; just believe." You can read about it in Mark 5. Jesus reacted immediately. He didn't want to give Jairus a chance to change his positive confession of faith spoken earlier. Don't change your confession.

Remember it also happened to Peter. There was a storm, and Jesus came walking to the disciples on the water. Peter wanted to try it and Jesus said, 'come on.' Peter stepped out of the boat and was doing just fine. Then Matthew 14:30-31 says, "But when he saw the wind, he was afraid and, beginning to sink, cried out, "Lord save me!" Immediately Jesus reached out his hand and caught him. "You of little faith," he said, "why did you doubt?" You see, it only took an instant. Peter took his eyes off Jesus and began to focus instead on the storm raging around him. What did the storm have to do with it anyway? Could Peter have walked on water any easier on a sunny day? The storm was only a distraction of the enemy. Sun or storm, we must stay focused on Jesus. Keep focused on what Jesus says, not on what you see. Satan will use your physical senses to deceive you. God's Word alone is the only reliable truth.

2 Corinthians 10:4-5

For the weapons of our warfare are not of the flesh, but divinely powerful for the destruction of fortresses. We are destroying speculations and every lofty thing raised up against the knowledge of God, and we are taking every thought captive to the obedience of Christ. (NASB)[40]

Paul tells us our battles are not in the physical realm. The real battle is happening in the spiritual realm. Spiritual laws supersede physical laws. The spiritual law of shalom will supersede the physical law of the curse (sickness and disease.) When you are fighting in the physical realm, you are at a distinct disadvantage because your enemy is fighting against you in the spiritual realm. If you intend to win, you must learn to fight on spiritual ground.

---

[40] Scripture taken from the New American Standard Bible ®, copyright 1960, 1962, 1963, 1968, 1971, 1972, 1973, 1975, 1977, 1995, by The Lockman Foundation. Used by permission.

Paul says we possess weapons having divine power by which we are able to 'kathairesis'[41] demolish, bring down, bring to extinction, crush, smash, and destroy every grip the enemy has on you. Paul says you must also demolish 'logismos'[42] or human reasonings. These are imaginations, ungodly thoughts, things you have elevated ahead of God, schemes of the enemy, and incorrect mental perceptions. We must make them obey the Anointed One and His anointing. Christ is not Jesus' last name. It is His title. It is the Greek equivalent of the Hebrew word Messiah, meaning the 'Anointed One.' You cannot separate the 'anointing' from the 'anointed one.' The anointing is the burden removing, yoke destroying power of God.

What are these weapons? They are exactly the same weapons Jesus used: faith, the Word, and the Holy Spirit. Paul outlines your armor in Ephesians chapter six which we will study in a moment.

Galatians 3:13-14

Christ redeemed us from the curse of the law by becoming a curse for us, for it is written: "Cursed is everyone who is hung on a tree." He redeemed us in order that the blessing given to Abraham might come to the Gentiles through Christ Jesus, so that by faith we might receive the promise of the Spirit.

As God's Anointed One (Christ), Jesus bore the entire curse of the law on Calvary's cross. The curse began in the

---

41 Thayer's Greek Lexicon, Strongs #G2506
42 Ibid, G3053

Garden of Eden and includes even death. Jesus ransomed us by paying the price of a life. His life for yours. You see, the law could only bring death because it was impossible for man to keep the law. The law given to Moses revealed God's character, His standard. The law gave man an opportunity to redeem Himself. God knew man couldn't do it alone, but man didn't realize it. There was nothing wrong with the law except for man's inability to keep it. It was intended to reveal man's need for a savior.

The law also provided temporary protection from the curse. As long as you kept the law, you lived in the blessing. Disobedience to the law left you open to the curse. However, when man failed, he could bring a substitute sacrifice for himself. The blood of the innocent animal would atone (cover over) his sin. These blood sacrifices foreshadowed the true deliverance by Messiah. Messiah's blood didn't cover over sin; it completely destroyed sin and the curse. The New Testament word is 'remit.' It means sin was put away or eradicated. Jesus blood provided a thorough cleansing. One drop of Jesus' blood will vaporize even the worst sin so that it no longer exists.

Everyone who accepts Jesus as their substitute, by faith, becomes righteous before God (in right standing). You gain the blessing of Abraham because you are grafted into the family, the chosen people of God. Abraham entered into a blood covenant with God. As covenant partners, all God has is now available to Abraham and his children. Guess what God has? Shalom. And you should know what shalom means by now. You should be renewing your mind to it.

We also received the indwelling presence of the third member of the trinity. Under the old covenant only three offices were anointed by the Holy Spirit: priests, prophets, or kings. No one else could carry the anointing. We now have a better covenant. Every believer receives the power of God within them (Romans 8:11).

Ephesians 6:13

Therefore put on the full armor of God, so that when the day of evil comes, you may be able to stand your ground, and after you have done everything, to stand.

Paul says put on all the armor of God. It is called the armor of God because it is supernatural armor. Don't miss any of the pieces because the enemy will come against you. That's a fact. When you begin to stand on God's Word, be prepared for a fight. Satan does not want you to grab hold of these truths and he will do whatever he can to dissuade you.

The full armor is listed in Ephesians 6:10-18. The loinbelt of Truth is the Word of God. God's Word is Truth. It is the most important piece because the loinbelt holds all the other pieces in place. The breastplate of righteousness declares God has made us righteous because of our position in Christ. Truly knowing this will enable you to operate confidently in faith. The shoes of peace declare peace with God. Knowing you have been reconciled to God is the solid foundation for your faith. A Roman soldier's war shoes had three inch spikes. It enabled the soldier to stand firmly on the ground. It also enable him to trample the fallen enemy underfoot. Your shield of faith needs to stay up. The helmet of salvation fits tightly to your head. It is the full knowledge of your salvation and everything it entails. Salvation is the whole benefit package.

The armor includes your offensive weapon – the sword of the spirit which is the Word of God. Wait a minute—I thought you said the loinbelt was the Word of Truth. It is. The sword is that Word coming out of your mouth. The Greek word 'rhema' is used for 'word.' It carries the idea of a quickened word, such as a Word of scripture or a direct word from the Lord. It is a specific word which the Holy Spirit quickens to your heart, at a specific time, for a specific purpose.

The armor gives you the ability to 'anthistemi'[43] stand against, withstand, resist and oppose the attacks, hardships, perils, and annoyances of the enemy. After you have done everything in God's Word (which is guaranteed to bring results) just STAND. Make a stand. Be immovable and fixed. Stand your ground. Don't give up. Keep doing it no matter what it looks like.

Hebrews 10:35

So do not throw away your confidence; it will be richly rewarded.

The word translated 'confidence' is 'parrhesia'[44]. It also means 'boldness' or 'assurance.' Hang on to what you know that you know. Be bold about it. In studying this Greek word I found another interesting concept. This word also refers to speech. It means to be publicly outspoken or unreserved in your speech. I believe it tells us to speak the Word in bold assurance even in the face of sickness and disease. Don't change your proclamation.

---

[43] Thayer's Greek Lexicon, Strongs #G436
[44] Ibid. G3954

God's Word says I am healed. Jesus bore my sickness and diseases and by His wounds I am healed. I don't care what it looks like. I don't care what I feel like. God's Word says I am healed. I believe God's Word. I speak God's Word and I will continue to speak God's Word until I see the full manifestation of it. Praise God!

If you maintain your bold assurance, God says you will be 'richly rewarded.' These words mean great abundance, something prepared on a grand scale. The word 'reward' is 'misthapodosia'[45] and means payment of wages due or recompense. In other words, your parrhesia (confidence) is running up a heavenly tab, and praise God you know He's good for the money. He will settle your account exceedingly, abundantly!

Hebrews 10:38

But my righteous one will live by faith.

Just as you received your salvation by faith, you also receive everything else in God's kingdom by faith. The whole thing works by faith. You see, it was Jesus who gave you the faith to ask Him into your heart (Hebrews 12:2). Faith has already been given to you. It is not something you need to pray for. You already have it. You do need to develop it. That is done by studying and meditating on God's Word until he gives you personal revelation knowledge on a particular subject. If you are trying to build your faith on healing, keep meditating on God's Word regarding healing. Once it drops from your head to your heart (inner man), its power is released. What does it

---

[45] Thayer's Greek Lexicon, Strongs #G3405

mean to meditate? It's simple. Just do what you do when you worry. You roll it over and over in your head. You speak the problem. You rehearse different scenarios in your mind. You mutter under your breath. Simply do that in reverse. Do it with what God's says instead of what the problem is.

Hebrews 11:1

Now faith is the substance of things hoped for, the evidence of things not seen (KJV)[46].

The word translated 'substance' (being sure) is 'hupostasis'[47] and means essence, substance, or confirmation. The Amplified translation says, "Now faith is the assurance (the confirmation, the title deed) of the things [we] hope for, being the proof of things [we] do not see and the conviction of their reality [faith perceiving as real fact what is not revealed to the senses][48]. Faith does not have to see the property because its already holding the title deed. Faith is assurance or belief.

Hope, in the Greek, does not mean 'wish.' It is an intense expectancy based upon trust. Hope grows out of trust in the Word of God and enables you to see the result in your mind's eye. This hope produces something tangible: faith, which produces the result before the proof can even be seen.

Our hope is based in the truthfulness of God's Word. The bible is more than an ink and paper recording of God's Word. God's Word IS God. God IS His Word. Therefore, the

---

[46] Scripture taken from the Holy Bible King James Version

[47] Thayer's Greek Lexicon, Strongs #G5287

[48] Scripture taken from the Amplified New Testament, copyright © 1954, 1958, 1987 by The Lockman Foundation. Used by permission.

bible IS God. It's not just a book about God. It IS God. John 1:1 says, "In the beginning was the Word and the Word was with God, and the Word was God." Verse 3 says, "Through him all things were made." So the Word of God, which Is God, created all things. It is God's power to call things into existence from nothing. God is His Word. There is life in the Word. Hebrews 4:12 says, "For the Word that God speaks is alive and full of power [making it active, operative, energizing, and effective]" (AMP)[49]. God's word is pregnant with the very life of God. Jesus said, "The words I have spoken to you are spirit and they are life" (John 6:63). 'Words' is 'rhemata'[50] the plural of 'rhema' as opposed to 'logos.' It is the Word with revelation/ enlightenment. The rhema/enlightened word is Spirit, 'pneuma' and 'zoe' (the very life force of God). What an awesome privilege God has given us to be able to put His Word in our mouth.

The things we hope for are things we are expecting. What are we expecting? Whatever God's Word says. If God's Word says you are healed, then that's what you are expecting. Remember, faith is the proof or the evidence of what you do not see. Faith already sees it as fact, in the spiritual realm. Remember, you are a spirit, you have a soul, and you live in a body. When you place your spirit in control, your physical body will eventually be forced to conform.

---

[49] Scripture taken from the Amplified New Testament, copyright © 1954, 1958, 1987 by The Lockman Foundation. Used by permission.
[50] Thayer's Greek Lexicon, Strongs #G4487

James 1:6-8

But when he asks, he must believe and not doubt, because he who doubts is like a wave of the sea, blown and tossed by the wind. That man should not think he will receive anything from the Lord; he is a double-minded man, unstable in all he does.

You must believe it's God's will to heal you. 1John 5:14-15 says, "This is the confidence we have in approaching God: that if we ask anything according to his will, he hears us. And if we know that he hears us – whatever we ask – we know that we have what we asked of him." If you know it's God's will, then you know it's already a done deal with God. Begin to thank Him whether you see the manifestation of it or not. Once you pray and ask God for your healing, it's done. After that, just continue confessing His Word about healing over your situation. Say, "No devil, I don't believe you. I received my healing. God says I'm healed." You can't say things like, "Well, if it's God's will to heal me, He will." Healing is either God's will or it isn't. Make up your mind.

Remember, the idea is to put your spirit-man in control. When you get enough of God's Word into your spirit, it will not matter if your mind (soul) has doubts. Doubt doesn't work in your mind anymore than faith does. The term 'double-minded' is an English term. The Greek word 'dipsuchos'[51] means two-spirited or vacillating. It causes a man to be unstable or inconsistent. Your mind and your feelings can do whatever they want to. Remember the Mark 11:23 passage? Jesus said not to doubt in your heart (that's your spirit). He

---

[51] Thayer's Greek Lexicon, Strongs #G1374

didn't say anything about what your mind was doing. You control the situation by your spirit. Don't speak out of your mind. Speak out of your spirit.

James 4:7

Submit yourselves, then, to God. Resist the devil, and he will flee from you.

Many people try to resist and rebuke devils without paying attention to the first part of this verse. It says, 'submit to God.' That means obedience to God and to His Word. Being submitted to the Word means believing you are healed because He said so. The word 'submit' means to subordinate oneself or to relinquish control. It is a Greek military term meaning 'under the command of a leader.' Does that mean if you sin you won't get your healing? That depends on you. We all fall short at times; but, thank God, He is merciful. However, if you are involved in active sin you must stop. Sin is a breach of the covenant. You can't stand on a covenant that you, yourself, are breaking. Confess the sin and ask forgiveness. Keep short accounts. As soon as the Holy Spirit makes you aware of sin, confess it immediately and ask forgiveness.

There is another key issue here. Lack of forgiveness toward others will also hinder your faith. God says, "For if you forgive men when they sin against you, your heavenly Father will also forgive you. But if you do not forgive men their sins, your Father will not forgive your sins" (Matthew 6:14-15). Please note that Jesus was not addressing salvation here. He was teaching believers to pray. Salvation is a free gift of God's grace. No one can do anything to earn it nor can they do anything to keep it. This is not a salvation issue. This is a practical issue. Lack of forgiveness will block God's power. You cannot be submitted to God and be in strife with others. Strife hinders faith. It's a spiritual principle. It blocks God's anointing. If I have an argument with my husband before I go to teach, I must settle it if I want God's anointing on my teaching. Otherwise, it will not be there. I've learned that. Reread Deception #4, in Chapter 4 for more information.

Once you are submitted to God, then you are in a position to resist. 'Resist' is the Greek word 'anthistemi'[52]. It is a verb (an action word) from which we get our English word antihistamine. The verb is in the imperative active aorist tense. It is a command to actively and immediately take your stand against the devil. It means drawing a line in the sand and saying, "No more devil, I'm taking my stand right here, right now. I'm not going to give you one inch of ground. The Word (my antihistamine) says I'm healed. I'm anti devil, anti-sickness, anti-disease and I oppose you and your work. I declare, decree and establish that I am healed." Not only must you resist to get healed, but you will also need to resist to stay healed. Eventually Satan will try to put those same old symptoms back on you. It's easier for Satan to convince you of a previous problem than a new one. He will try to get you to doubt your healing. Many people lose their healing this way. When it happens, watch your words. If you say, "Well I thought I was healed, but I guess I'm not," that's an engraved invitation for Satan to come and put that old thing back on you.

---

[52] Thayer's Greek Lexicon, Strongs#G436

The bible says resist, resist, resist, and keep resisting. Hit the enemy with the truth. Quote the Word, quote the Word, quote the Word, and he will flee from you.

James 5:14-15

Is any one of you sick? He should call the elders of the church to pray over him and anoint him with oil in the name of the Lord. And the prayer offered in faith will make the sick person well; the Lord will raise him up. If he has sinned he will be forgiven.

"Is any one of you sick?" James was writing this to believers. I believe James was saying, 'If there is, there shouldn't be. Believers are delivered from sickness. Every one of them should be walking in health. If they are not, bring them here and get them healed! Anoint them and pray over them. Perhaps they don't understand how to achieve healing for themselves.'

Isaiah prophesied about the Millennial Kingdom of Messiah's rule and reign. He said the same thing. *"No one living in Zion will say, 'I am ill'; and the sins of those who dwell there will be forgiven* (Isaiah 33:24).

Look at the scripture in James again. What makes the sick person well? Does it say the anointing with oil will make them well? No. It says, the 'prayer offered in FAITH' will make them well. The Greek text says the prayer offered in faith will save 'sozo'[53] the sick. 'Sozo' is the Greek equivalent to the Hebrew word 'shalom.' It means save, deliver, heal, protect, make whole. It goes on to say, "And the Lord will raise him

---

[53] Thayer's Greek Lexicon, Strongs #G4982

up." The word 'raise' is 'egeiro'[54] and means to waken or rouse from sleeping, death, sickness or ruin. To cause to stand up again.

So what does the anointing oil do? I'm glad you asked. Some people are not yet developed in their faith. For example, you cannot expect a brand new believer to have developed their faith for healing. The oil, representing the Holy Spirit, is a point of contact for a believer giving them something tangible to focus on and helping them to understanding something is happening in the spiritual realm. It enables them to have a point of release for their faith. Mature believers are expected to come along side and believe with them through the prayer of faith. When mature believers follow this command to anoint with oil and pray, they are not to be 'sin conscious.' If disobedience has opened a door for the enemy to attack that person, God says, He will forgive them and they will be healed. What a great God we serve. He has done His best to provide healing and restoration for everyone. If we aren't receiving, it's not God's fault.

If you are just beginning in your walk of faith, get yourself into a church that believes in healing. Submit yourself to that pastor and get your healing this way. Do not hesitate to call for the elders of the church.

1 Peter 2:24

He himself bore our sins in his body on the tree so that we might die to sins and live for righteousness; by his wounds you have been healed.

---

[54] Thayer's Greek Lexicon, Strongs #G1453

Like the scapegoat in Leviticus chapter sixteen, God laid all the sins of the world on Jesus. The word 'bore' is 'anaphero'[55] which means to carry, to bring up, or to offer up. Jesus paid the full penalty so man could be restored to Adam's condition before the fall. A fully righteous condition and restored fellowship with God. Sin and all its consequences have been abolished.

The word we have translated 'healed' is 'iaomai'[56] and means to heal, to cure, to make whole. Does that sound familiar. It also reminds me of the Hebrew word 'shalom.' Nothing missing, nothing broken. Did you also notice the past tense verbs? Jesus purchased our healing two thousand years ago. Don't you think it's time to act like it?

1 Peter 5:7

Cast all your anxiety on him because he cares for you.

God tells His people many times throughout scripture not to fear. Jesus also told his followers not to worry. He didn't say, 'try not to worry.' He said, "Do not worry." It's a command. Our God understands how faith works. Worrying reveals your lack of confidence in God. There is no problem or person whom God cannot handle. He has provided the way out for you. The answers are in His Word. He has done everything He can do. You must act on His Word in faith. Worry is fear. In the spirit realm, fear works exactly the opposite of faith. They are both spiritual laws. Fear empowers Satan in the same way faith empowers God.

---

[55] Thayer's Greek Lexicon, Strongs #G399
[56] Ibid. G2390

He says, lay all your care 'merimna'[57] at His feet. This Greek word carries the idea of distraction. Cares, concerns, and worries are distractions from your faith and from God's plan for your life. No matter how big, no matter how small, just say, "I'm not going to worry about this. I'm giving it to you Lord Jesus. I declare 'Jesus is Lord' in this situation. I'm going to find out what your Word has to say about this situation, and I'm going to trust your Word." Then begin praising God in spite of the situation. Praising God takes your mind off the problem and re-focuses it on God's ability to intervene.

---

[57] Thayer's Greek Lexicon, Strongs #G3308

CHAPTER SEVEN

DAILY MEDICINE

It is vitally important to meditate God's Word. Then you can pray God's Word from your heart. Continue to meditate the Word until you get a picture on the inside of you. God told Joshua to meditate on His Word day and night. To meditate in the Hebrew means to mutter under your breath, to ponder, to imagine, to talk and to utter.

Joshua 1:8

Do not let this Book of the Law depart from your mouth; meditate on it day and night, so that you may be careful to do everything written in it. Then you will be prosperous and successful.

You need to put God's Words before your eyes every day. Speak them out loud so your ears can hear them. Memorize them. There is a point where you get so much of God's word into your spirit that it makes a transition. It passes from being mere intellectual knowledge to becoming true heart knowledge. When you can see that picture on the inside of you, then you can pray and it becomes the fervent, heartfelt prayer mentioned in James 5:16 that become effectual (or dynamic) in its working. Its power is released and it shall come to pass. As you meditate, ask the Father to give you revelation knowledge about the scripture you are meditating. You cannot short cut the process. God's Word is not a voodoo book. You can't just quote verses like magical spells and incantations. God's Word requires a relationship with Him. He is the healer. Your faith must be in Him speaking to you through His Word. Your faith is the hook-up to His anointing. It is still His anointing. This is not something you can manufacture on your own. His Words work because He is backing them.

Knowledge imparted to me will not help you. Meditate on these verses. Pray to God about them. Keep them before your eyes. Keep them coming out of your mouth. God will be faithful to give you personal revelation knowledge of them. When God imparts revelation knowledge to you, a light will come on inside your sprit. Then His Word coming out of your mouth explodes in power!

The best way to use God's Word for healing is to get it in there BEFORE you get sick. Staying in God's Word will actually ward off sickness and disease. Sometimes it's a matter of rebuking symptoms as quick as they start. If you sneeze, don't say, "Oh no, I must be getting a cold." That's an open invitation! Instead, say, "Praise God, I'm so glad Jesus purchased my healing 2000 years ago. I'm the healed of the Lord." Always be on guard. Don't give the enemy a foothold.

If you have been sick for a while, don't be discouraged if the manifestation of your healing doesn't happen immediately. In many cases, people have waited so long before coming to God's Word that the enemy has done a lot of damage. Allow your faith to grow and repair the damage. Don't give up. Walk by faith, not by sight. Those words of faith may have to rebuild an area in your body cell by cell. That may take some time. Never, never step back from God's Word once you begin. By the same token, it shouldn't take years to receive your healing either. The word says:

Then your light will break forth like the dawn, and your healing will quickly appear.

(Isaiah 58:8)

Jesus said:

And will not God bring about justice for his chosen ones, who cry out to him day and night? Will he keep putting them off? I tell you, he will see that they get justice, and quickly. However, when the Son of Man comes, will he find faith on the earth?"

(Luke 18:7-8)

If you have been confessing God's Word on healing for six months to a year and you're not making any progress, go to God. If it's not working, it's not God's Word that's the problem. It's something else. You will need to get the wisdom of God on the issue. There may be something you're missing. The best way to receive God's wisdom on a particular issue is to make a commitment to receive it. Make a commitment to fast and pray until you receive the answer. Get alone with God at every opportunity for several days in a row. Pray in the spirit about it. As you pray release out of your mouth whatever the Holy Spirit brings into your spirit. Don't pray about anything else. Focus on that one issue until God gives you His wisdom on it. It won't take long. God is faithful. He does not hide anything from those who diligently seek Him. Listen to what Jesus' brother James said about seeking wisdom:

If any of you lacks wisdom, he should ask God, who gives generously to all without finding fault, and it will be given to him.

(James 1:5)

There may be some unconfessed sin at fault. There may be some habit you need to change before your healing can manifest. God will give you wisdom. Jesus said,

And ye shall know the truth, and the truth shall make you free.
(John 8:32 KJV[58])

Trust in God. Keep the Word in front of your eyes. Keep the Word going into your ears. Keep the Word coming out of your mouth. Jesus said, "I am the truth," and He walked on water to prove truth is superior to natural facts. Glory to God, the Truth will overcome the facts!

---

[58] Scripture taken from The Holy Bible King James Version

PRAYERS

SALVATION PRAYER

If you have never asked Jesus into your heart and would like to do so now, pray this prayer from your heart.

Father God, I recognize that I am a sinner. Your Word says in Romans 3:23, "for all have sinned and fall short of the glory of God." But your Word also says in John 3:16, "For God so loved the world that he gave his one and only Son that whoever believes in him shall not perish but have eternal life." Lord, Jesus I believe you died for my sin. I don't want to be a stranger to you anymore. I want my relationship with you to be restored. I'm inviting you to come into my heart right now. I believe God raised you from the dead to show me that the enemy has been completely defeated.

I thank you Father that I now have the assurance of eternal life. My spirit has been reborn! I am a Christian. I am now your child. (1John 3:1-2, 5:1) I have been adopted into the Covenant family of Abraham (Galatians 3:6). I thank you for the inheritance I am now entitled to under this covenant (Ephesians 1:18).

Find a good church where they preach the Word of God and faith. Ask to be baptized. It is the Lord's command to us (Matthew 28:19-20). Baptism is an outward sign of your new faith in Jesus. It signifies your burial with Him in death and your resurrection to new life. It also expresses the fact of your deliverance from the curse and habits of this world. It is a public statement to others and to the enemy that you have crossed over to the promised land of God's kingdom.

If you have prayed this prayer, write to me and I will send you a free booklet to help you on your new journey of faith. I rejoice at having new sisters and brothers in the Lord's family.

For information about faith churches in your area:

The International Convention of Faith Ministries (ICFM)
(817) 451-9620
5500 Woodland Park Blvd., Arlington, TX 76013.
www.ICFM.org. Click on ICFM Members.

Andrew Wommack Ministries
awmi.net
Click on the 'About Tab' then 'Our Ministries'
then 'Associated Ministries'

Kenneth Hagin Ministries
Rhema Bible Training College
rhema.org Click on: Find a Rhema Church

PRAYER FOR THE BAPTISM OF THE HOLY SPIRIT

Father God, Your word says that on the day I became a born-again believer your Spirit came to dwell inside of me and marked me with a seal as your child (John 14:15-17 & 2 Corinthians 1:22).

Father I am now asking for the anointing power of the baptism of the Holy Spirit. I receive it by faith just as I received my salvation by faith. Your word says in Luke 11:13, "If you then, though you are evil, know how to give good gifts to your children, how much more will your Father in heaven give the Holy Spirit to those who ask him." Father, Your Word says, "You will receive power when the Holy Spirit comes on you" (Acts 1:8).

Holy Spirit, rise up within me. I fully expect to speak with other tongues as You give me utterance (Acts 2:4).

As you begin to praise God, you will begin to feel syllables and words rising up from your Spirit. They will sound foreign to your ears because this is a special language given you by the Holy Spirit. Let them come out. You must do the speaking. The Holy Spirit is not speaking. The believer speaks as the Spirit gives him utterance.

God's Word tells us that by the Spirit we speak the mysteries of God. We can use our prayer language to speak to God and to edify ourselves. To edify means to build up. It is like charging a battery (1 Corinthians 14:2-4). It gives you the ability to pray in the perfect will of God (Romans 8:26-27). Pray in the Spirit every day. This keeps your spirit strong. I believe there are certain breakthroughs with healing that will never manifest unless they are prayed out in the Spirit. There are many things (mysteries) we do not understand, but we have been given a powerful resource to unveil those mysteries. As you pray in the Spirit, a scripture or statement may rise up from your spirit. It is vitally important to release it immediately by speaking it out. Stay with those things until you get the victory. There are certain things that the Holy Spirit wants released at key times to break through strongholds in the spiritual realm. Remember, the Holy Spirit can only draw out of you as much Word as you have taken the time to put into your heart. Be diligent in God's Word. God bless you as you grow in the Spirit.

How to Order

....

God's Healing Medicine
Daily Scriptures For Faith and Miracles

Paperback or Ebook
Available on Amazon.com

If you have enjoyed this book, help others by
submitting a positive review on Amazon.

....

FREE OFFER

Join the email list for future offers and receive
a free PDF Article "Melchizedek, King of
Righteousness"

Discover who Melchizedek really was!

Email Covenant Freelance Services at:
CFS.AZ.JMB@gmail.com.

Put "Join" in the Subject line. In the body, tell
us where you obtained this book.

www.ingramcontent.com/pod-product-compliance
Lightning Source LLC
Chambersburg PA
CBHW071455070426
42452CB00040B/1366